Loc
Av

k
vay

Text by Paul Sherman

Dedication

For my family, Kelly, Lila, and Nora.
As you go through life, never look away!

For my parents, Alice and Ed, who supported
this book from beginning to end.

and

For all my Kickstarter backers. Thank you.

Book design: adamhaystudio.com

Cover photography by Willie Stark.

Photography credits for the interior of the book are listed
on page 175, which serves as a supplement to this page.

For information about bulk purchases, special editions, or
excerpts, please contact sales@xparkpress.com. The author is
available for speaking and book readings. For more information,
please contact speaking@xparkpress.com

First published by Paul Sherman in 2017

ISBN: 978-0-9992472-6-6
ISBN: 978-0-9992472-7-3 (ebook)

Introduction

by Paul Sherman

Fifteen minutes after Hillary Clinton placed her concession call to Donald Trump, the world watched and waited as the new president-elect slowly descended the stairs from the balcony overlooking his victory party. Trump, his family, and his closest advisors walked single file down a short runway toward the stage as music boomed through the hotel ballroom. Just before reaching the podium, he stopped and posed with his wife and children around an unusual prop: a glass display case with a red "Make America Great Again" hat inside of it.

The elevation of the red hat by the Trump campaign is understandable. "Make America Great Again" will likely go down in American history as one the most influential political slogans, along with Lincoln's "Don't Change Horses in Midstream," Eisenhower's "I Like Ike," and Obama's "Hope." Historians have already speculated that the original red hat will end up at the Smithsonian Institution or a future Trump Presidential Library.

However, sexist, crude, and racist messages also played an important role on the campaign trail. Vulgar slogans were pervasive on unofficial campaign materials distributed around Trump rallies. It wasn't uncommon to see a merchant selling "Make America Great Again" hats next to a stack of "Trump that Bitch" bumper stickers. Before 2016, such items would have been unthinkable at a major presidential nominee's rally.

Sexist, crude, and racist messages played an important role on the campaign trail. Vulgar slogans were pervasive on unofficial campaign materials distributed around Trump rallies.

The coarse and sexist Trump items tell an important story about the 2016 campaign. They were tangible, touchable proof that the country's political discourse had broken from the past.

As a collector of political items for the past 35 years, with drawers full of political memorabilia from past campaigns, I was watching the election closely in 2016. As I do every four years, I collected political items from all the major candidates. In pursuit of political paraphernalia, I visited campaign field offices, attended many rallies, and traveled to both the Democratic and Republican national conventions. As the campaign progressed, I kept returning to the Trump items; I ended up collecting and documenting hundreds of them. The coarse and sexist Trump items tell an important story about the 2016 campaign. They were tangible, touchable proof that the country's political discourse had broken from the past.

I started collecting political buttons, signs, and bumper stickers with my father when I was a child growing up in Austin, Texas, during the 1980s. Late on many election nights, we would head out on a collector's expedition. After the polls closed we would pick up campaign signs at polling locations, and we would occasionally drop in on official victory parties. We amassed stacks of campaign signs from a wide range of candidates in our garage – Carter, Reagan, Mondale, Bush, and more – along with many older campaign buttons, some dating back 125 years.

Carrying on my family's collecting tradition, I took my nine-year-old daughter, who had just started her own political button collection, to a Trump rally in Leesburg, Virginia. It was her first political rally, just two nights before Election Day. Memories of my early collecting days were running through my mind as we approached the entrance to the Loudoun 4H Fairgrounds in Leesburg, Virginia, where Trump would speak five hours later.

Floodlights illuminated the evening sky as a large crowd assembled near the entrance to the Fairgrounds. People were snapping photos in front of a vintage green U.S. Army cargo truck with a Trump-Pence sign mounted on top. Heavily armed security officers patrolled the perimeter. The entrance had a festive feeling, almost like the hour before a Fourth of July fireworks show. A few tables covered with Trump shirts stood next to sheriff trucks that flanked the entrance to the Fairgrounds. Merchants were holding up "Make America Great Again" hats for sale.

As we waited in the long line that snaked back and forth for over a mile, a few hawkers sold shirts with bloody and ghoulish images of Hillary. A woman wearing a Hillary mask, an orange jumpsuit, and handcuffs posed with attendees for selfies. A man wore a "Hillary Killed My Friends" sticker on his shirt, a reference to the Benghazi attacks. Despite the long wait, which was common at most Trump rallies, the crowd was in good spirits, excited about the massive turnout and hopeful the enthusiasm would spill over to Election Day. The vendors, as usual, were providing some distraction. Occasionally, groups of people in line would spontaneously chant "Lock Her Up" or "Build the Wall." At this point it was a pretty conventional Trump pre-rally. This was my sixth Trump event; I had seen it all before.

Negative political items date back to the 19th century. Before the 2016 presidential campaign, they were often humorous and mocking in tone. The crudest buttons of the past were hidden in the fringes; campaigns generally wanted nothing to do with them at their carefully orchestrated rallies. As a kid, I thought an anti-FDR button that read "Eleanor Start Packing, the Wilkies Are Coming" in my father's collection was pretty tough stuff. And one of the most negative items I collected during the 1984 election was an anti-Reagan button that read, "No Mo'Ron for President". These items almost seem quaint compared to the buttons and T-shirts I saw at Trump rallies.

Early during the 2016 Republican primary, there were hints of the sexist and brutal items that ultimately became pervasive in the final months of the campaign. At a Trump rally in New Hampshire in February, when the Republican primary was still very much in play, a supporter held up a "Trump that Bitch" bumper sticker in the middle of the crowd, visible to Trump and the media. Trump squinted from behind his podium, read the sticker, and said, "This can

The crudest buttons of the past were hidden in the fringes. As a kid, I thought an anti-FDR button that read "Eleanor Start Packing, the Willkies Are Coming" in my father's collection was pretty tough stuff.

These items weren't part of the fringe. They were commonplace and part of the fabric of the rallies. They provided an element of entertainment for supporters waiting in long lines.

only happen at a Trump rally." A minute later, he returned to the sticker again, joking he would probably be criticized by the media for condoning the sticker. With a mock officious voice, he said, "Sir, you're reprimanded." He then quickly added, "But we aren't throwing him out folks." The audience roared.

After Trump cleared the Republican field, the misogynistic and vulgar merchandise was in full bloom. "Trump that Bitch," "Hillary for Prison," "Life's a Bitch, Don't Vote for One," "Monica Sucks, But Not Like Hillary," "Finally Someone with Balls," and "Don't Be a Pussy, Vote for Trump" were some of the common slogans on Trump merchandise. Homemade signs often depicted Hillary Clinton in anguish behind prison bars or in handcuffs. These items weren't part of the fringe. They were commonplace and part of the fabric of the rallies. They provided an element of entertainment and humor for supporters waiting in long lines. The items also signaled that the event they were about to attend, like the Trump campaign, would unabashedly break the traditional norms of campaigning. It is inconceivable that such items would have been commonplace at a Romney or McCain or Bush or Reagan rally. I have no doubt they would have been considered an embarrassment and a political liability to past presidential campaigns, quickly extinguished by campaign advance staff.

Sellers at Trump rallies would usually set up just outside the security ring of the arenas, amphitheaters, county fairgrounds, convention centers, and airport hangars where events were often held. Some would work the line, selling their merchandise and occasionally yelling the content of their T-shirts and buttons. The sellers of "Monica Sucks, But Not Like Hillary" shirts were notorious for their chants, and they would often get laughs from those in line. Some sellers would station their fold-up tables along the snaking lines, while others would assemble make-shift booths off the backs of SUVs in nearby parking lots.

It wasn't just political collectors who noticed something different with the Trump merchandise early in the campaign. Reporters on the campaign trail started covering it as news. "Trump Supporters Are Selling 'Trump That Bitch' T-Shirts Featuring Hillary Clinton" read a headline from Fortune. "Inside a Donald Trump Rally: The Nasty, Sexist, Racist Chants by His Supporters" read a headline on the People magazine website. Candace Smith of ABC News, one of the only black reporters covering the Trump campaign, started a hashtag, #ConfederateFlagsAcrossAmerica, to document Confederate flags she saw at Trump rallies.

The Trump campaign claimed it had no control over what vendors sold or what supporters brought into events. Campaign staffers sometimes would try to remove Confederate flags hanging inside rallies, but nobody bothered the vendors selling the flags outside or supporters wearing Confederate flag gear. At other times, the campaign just looked away and said it didn't see what the press was reporting. When The Washington Post's Jenna Johnson asked Trump in an interview about the T-shirts, buttons, and supporters calling Hillary Clinton a "bitch," he responded, "A bitch? No, I haven't heard that."

The Trump campaign relied heavily on its website for selling official merchandise. At many rallies, supporters were left to purchase gear from the independent sellers. But even the Trump website sold items that during past elections would have been unprecedented, including "Hillary Clinton for Prison" buttons, bumper stickers with the words "Rotten," "Liar," and "Crooked," and signs with distorted caricatures of Hillary Clinton.

At about the same time that the vulgar merchandise started appearing frequently, the campaign was actively trying to prevent protesters from entering its rallies. Campaign staff and local party operatives were watching the audience closely, trying to detect potential disrupters by examining the content of their shirts, buttons, hats, and signs. People wearing "Black Lives Matter" T-shirts or any message deemed anti-Trump were ordered to leave with a security escort or not allowed to enter. Individuals wearing crude, sexist, racist, and violent shirts –

Individuals wearing crude, sexist, racist, and violent shirts were almost always allowed to stay, and sometimes became a major draw for photos by attendees and the media.

Once the campaign was over, Trump seemed to applaud his supporters' tactics. "You were nasty and mean and vicious and you wanted to win," he said.

one man wore a "Hillary is a Cunt" shirt at a rally that went viral on Twitter – were almost always allowed to stay, and they sometimes became a major draw for photos by attendees and the media.

In late October, I attended a Trump rally in Virginia Beach on the campus of Regent University, the evangelical Christian university founded by Pat Robertson. As I walked across the campus and passed the Christian Broadcasting Network headquarters building, I saw one vendor selling buttons of the cartoon character Calvin, from Calvin and Hobbes, urinating on the word "Hillary." During a speech in front of the stately red-brick university library, a supporter held up a head of Hillary Clinton on a stake. Others held up shooting targets with Hillary Clinton's face in the middle of cross-hairs. One vendor sold a bumper sticker that declared the country needed a president "with a cock." At the end of the rally, I bought buttons that read "Fuck Mainstream Media" and "Lock Her Up and Throw Away the Key." The vendors were just feet from the Secret Service tent, legally set up on the campus of one of the most prominent Christian institutions in the country.

Once the campaign was over, Trump seemed to applaud his supporters' tactics. With Christmas trees as his backdrop, he told supporters in Orlando during one of his Thank You Tour events in December that he was aware of what was going on in the crowds. "You people were vicious, violent, screaming 'Where's the wall? We want the wall,'" he said. "You were nasty and mean and vicious and you wanted to win."

After waiting in line for over two hours at the Fairgrounds, my daughter and I were within sight of the security screening tent. We could see the main hall, called the "Barn," where the speech would be held. Thousands of people were still waiting behind barricades around the Fairgrounds, unable to get in because the event had reached capacity. Just before the tent stood the Jack Brown Pavilion. During the previous year's annual fair, the small Pavilion housed an Oreo stacking contest and a hypnotist show; this evening it housed tables offering "Bomb the Shit Out of ISIS" and "Trump that Bitch" buttons, along with other items mocking Hillary Clinton's health.

This evening, I noticed something different at the Pavilion that I hadn't noticed in previous events. These were authorized vendors. They certainly couldn't be called unauthorized. They had been granted permission to set up shop inside the Fairgrounds, which was within a massive security ring. The campaign's argument that these merchants were "unofficial" or "unauthorized" would not hold up this evening.

Over the course of a year, I talked to dozens of the vendors working on the Trump campaign. They were a varied group. Some had quit their jobs to sell merchandise exclusively at Trump rallies, while others had been hired by T-shirt producers to sell their goods. Some only sold within a limited geographic area, while others followed the campaign all around the country. Several vendors also sold items at concerts, sporting events, and gun shows. Most of them were entrepreneurial, making good money on the Trump caravan, and they had a knack for knowing what would sell. Some were true believers and supporters of Trump, while others opposed him and were just in it for the money. In the end, they were all entrepreneurial – they sold what the market wanted.

Had Trump wanted to scale back the presence of vendors selling vulgar material, he had many methods at his disposal. Political advance team staffers are skilled at just this kind of activity. The campaign clearly had leverage over the vendors. Most were operating without local business permits on the sidewalks and parking lots outside the rally venues. Elaborate security preparations brought together various law enforcement agencies before each rally, and advance teams could have requested that vendors be restricted or kept in designated areas.

"The Trump people take care of us," one vendor, who worked nearly 100 rallies and sold plenty of vulgar items, told me. He said campaign staffers sometimes tipped him off about the locations of upcoming rallies before they

Had Trump wanted to scale back the presence of vendors selling this type of material, he had many methods at his disposal. Political advance team staffers are skilled at just this kind of activity.

"The Trump people take care of us," one vendor, who worked nearly 100 rallies and sold plenty of vulgar items, told me.

were made public. The merchants' primary concern was with aggressive local authorities who occasionally wouldn't let them set up in public spaces. Some of the larger vendors had names, banners and painted vehicles that gave the appearance of an affiliation with the Trump campaign, such as "The Trump Store." Most sold knock-off, unofficial "Make America Great Again" hats and shirts that could have easily resulted in a trademark violation lawsuit by the Trump campaign, something Trump alluded to various times. These items were huge sellers. Corey Lewandowski, the former campaign manager, told CNN that Trump estimated eight out of every ten "Make America Great Again" hats that he signed after his speeches were knockoffs.

The campaign did use its leverage a few times. The Trump Organization sent an anti-Trump online store a "cease and desist" letter, claiming it was infringing on the Trump trademark. It also sent letters to the Ted Cruz and Scott Walker campaigns for their use of the trademarked "Make America Great Again" slogan. But they had a hands-off approach to the pro-Trump vendors, who became part of the color and vibe of the events.

My daughter and I finally made it to the Barn, which was jammed with over 2,000 people. Anticipation was growing in the crowd after the long wait. Voting on Election Day would start in Dixville Notch, New Hampshire, in less than 24 hours. Just after midnight on Monday morning, Trump's motorcade arrived to massive cheers. The crowd went wild when he took the stage. Trump opened the event by saying, "Hillary right now is fast asleep. She is sleeping so beautifully." This was Trump's sixth event of the day, and he generally followed the script from his previous stump speeches, touching on all the hot-button issues. After 1:00 in the morning, it was over. We had collected a few signs, stickers, and voter guides for our collections.

As we neared the exit, I heard a group of teenage boys laughing and giving high-fives to each other as they held up a shirt they had just purchased. One of them read the text on the shirt; the others burst out laughing. I had seen a lot of vulgar and sexist items this campaign – in fact I thought I had seen almost all of them – but I wasn't sure if I had heard him correctly.

I made my way through the crowd to the stacks of shirts on the tables. There it was. A shirt I had not seen at any Trump rally.

It read: "Trump: Grab'Em By the Pussy".

I took a photo of the shirt while simultaneously trying to block my daughter from seeing it. A lady next to me gave a noticeable gasp as she noticed my daughter trying to poke her head around me to read the shirt. The merchant looked up, saw my young daughter in her purple winter hat, and quickly flipped the shirt over, before she could read it.

The photo I took of the shirt is the blurriest one in this book, but it is also the most important to me. At the moment when I took the photo, I knew that what I and others had collected at Trump campaign rallies needed to be documented and remembered. These images could not remain buried in a drawer.

This book is the result.

I heard a group of teenage boys laughing and giving high-fives to each other as they held up a shirt they had just purchased. One of them read the text on the shirt; the others burst out laughing.

Pri

As "Make America Great Again" goes down in history as the leading slogan of the Trump campaign, "Hillary for Prison" will probably be remembered for its supporting role. "Lock Her Up" was the preferred chant at rallies, but it was "Hillary for Prison" that was widely printed on signs, T-shirts, bumper stickers, and just about any other type of gear. Images of handcuffs, prison jumpsuits, jail bars, and chains – sometimes with a photo of an anguished Hillary Clinton – often went along with the words. At many rallies, individuals would dress up in prison jumpsuits and wear Hillary masks. The message was endorsed and spread by the Trump campaign. The online store run by the Trump campaign and the Republican National Committee sold "Hillary Clinton for Prison 2017" buttons. During the second presidential debate, when Clinton said it was good that Trump was not overseeing the country's laws, Trump replied sternly, "Because you'd be in jail."

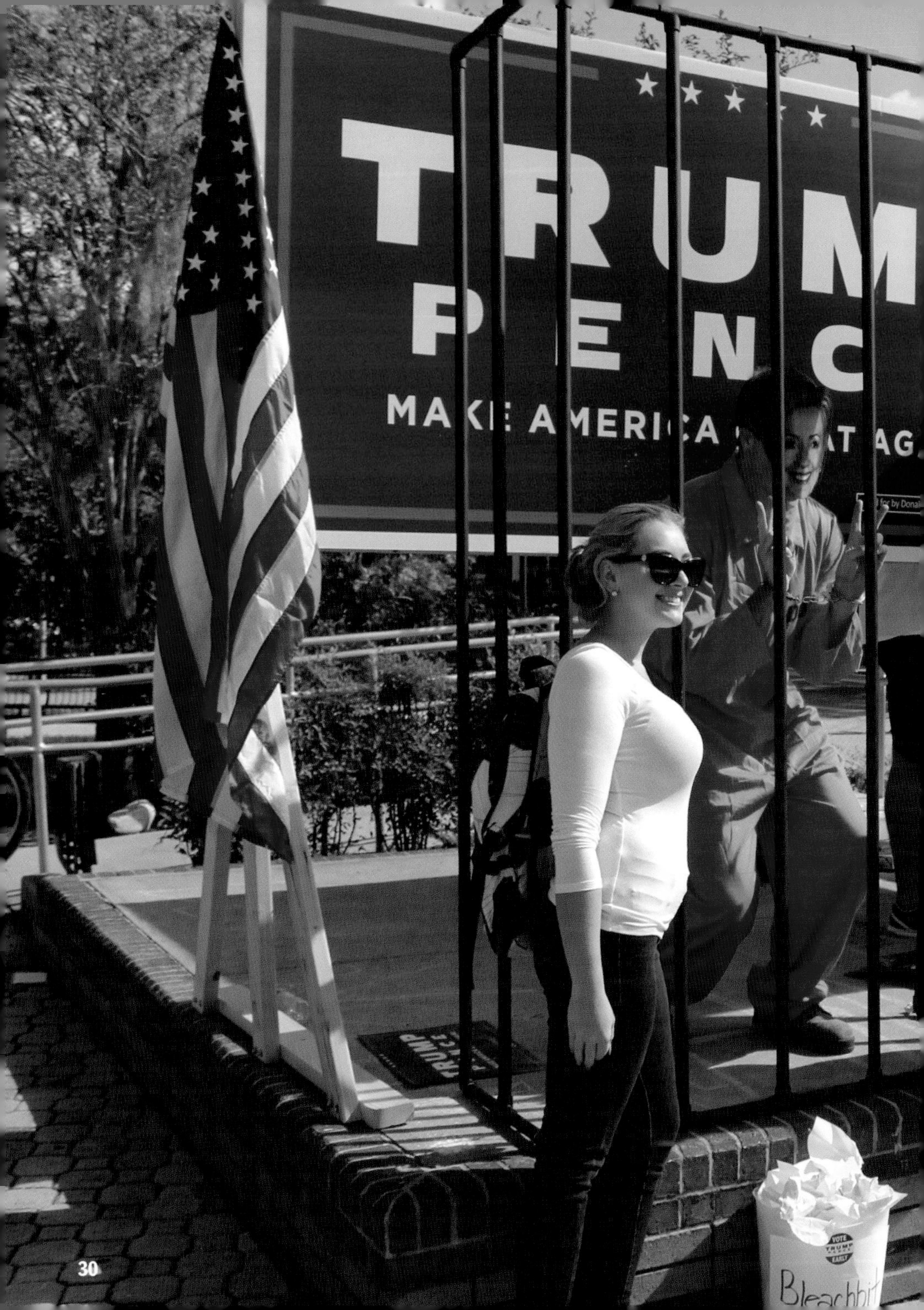
TRUM
PENC
MAKE AMERICA
TRUMP
Bleachbit

BIKERS FOR
TRUMP

Hillary
for Prison
2016

TRUMP
MAKE AMERICA GREAT AGAIN!

TRUMP
KE AMERICA GREAT AGAIN!

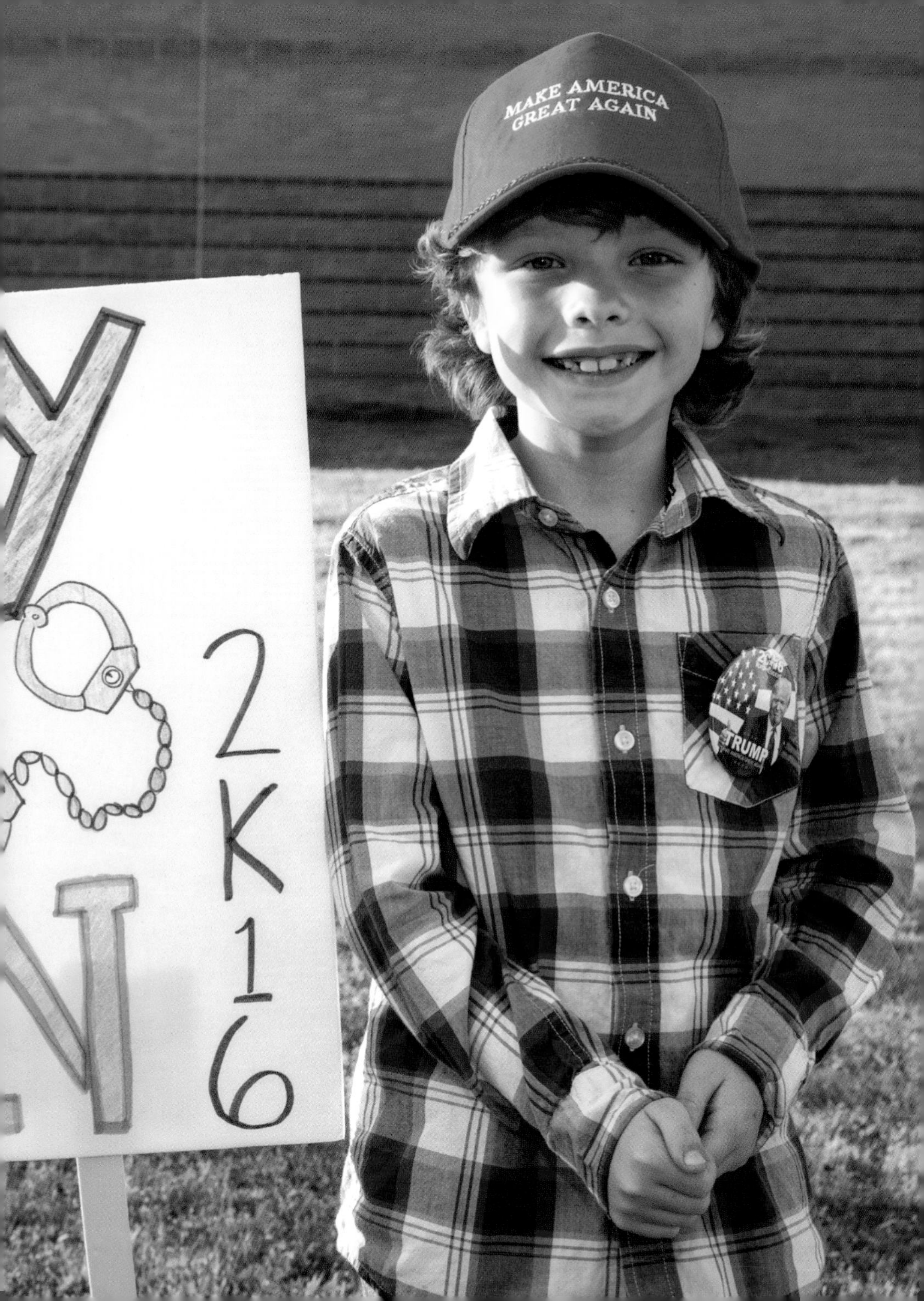
MAKE AMERICA
GREAT AGAIN
2K16
TRUMP

Bit

Throughout the 2016 election, the first woman presidential nominee of a major party was commonly referred to as "bitch" or "the bitch" or "that bitch" on unofficial Trump merchandise. It was acceptable for Trump supporters to wear "Trump that Bitch" or "Life is a Bitch, Don't Vote for One" shirts and buttons at his rallies. One of the more popular T-shirts featured a drawing of Trump on a motorcycle and a shocked Hillary Clinton falling off. Trump's motorcycle jacket read, "If you can read this, the bitch fell off." The bitch term was commonly yelled out during Trump events. At one rally in Ashburn, Virginia, a young boy shouted, "Take that Bitch Down!" as Trump was speaking. When reporters asked his mother about her son's language, she said, "I think he has a right to speak what he wants."

HILLARY
FOR
JAIL
...merica Great Again

TRUMP
THAT
BITCH

We The People
WANT OUR COUNTRY BACK!
TRUMP/PENCE

VIOLATORS WILL
BE TICKETED UNDER
ORDINANCE 43573

Vo
N

MORE

PRO

Viol

Many items sold outside Trump rallies depicted violence and abuse, primarily against Hillary Clinton. Shooting targets with Hillary Clinton's face in the crosshairs were popular in the final weeks of the campaign, and rally attendees held up these targets as Trump spoke. One shirt on sale showed Trump standing over a knocked-out Hillary Clinton in a boxing ring. Models of Hillary Clinton's bloody head on a stick or in a noose were displayed at some rallies. Other merchandise referenced waterboarding Hillary or sending her to Guantanamo. Violent messages were also directed against the press. One shirt that went viral on Twitter said, "Rope. Tree. Journalist. Some Assembly Required." In many ways, the acceptance of "Lock Her Up" and "Hillary for Prison" from the official campaign became a gateway to more violent imagery and language from supporters.

ence

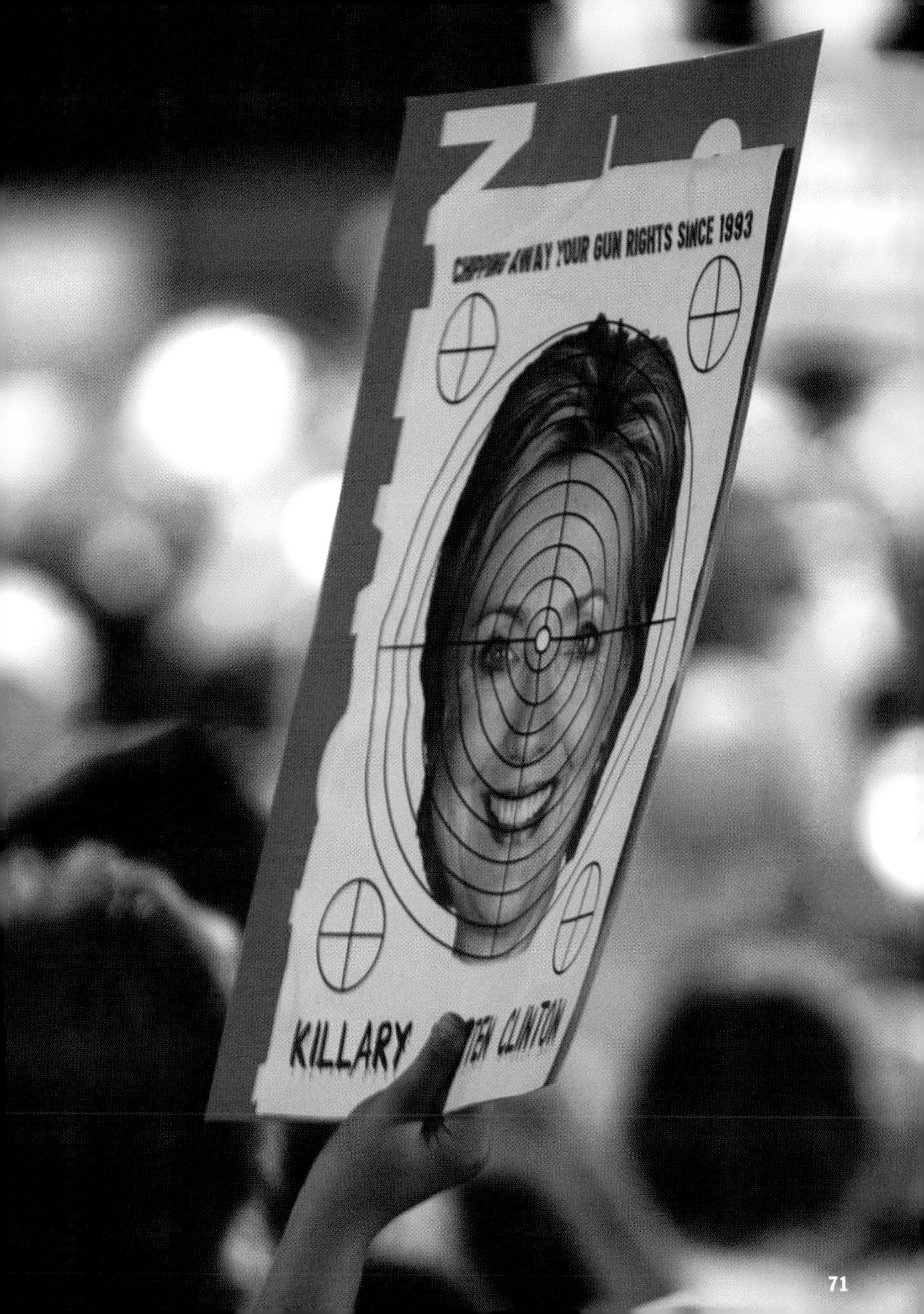
AWAY YOUR GUN RIGHTS SINCE 1993
KILLARY
CLINTON

'The Lyin' Hillary Doll'™

Item # A6073

www.lyinhillarydoll.com

PRESS
HERE

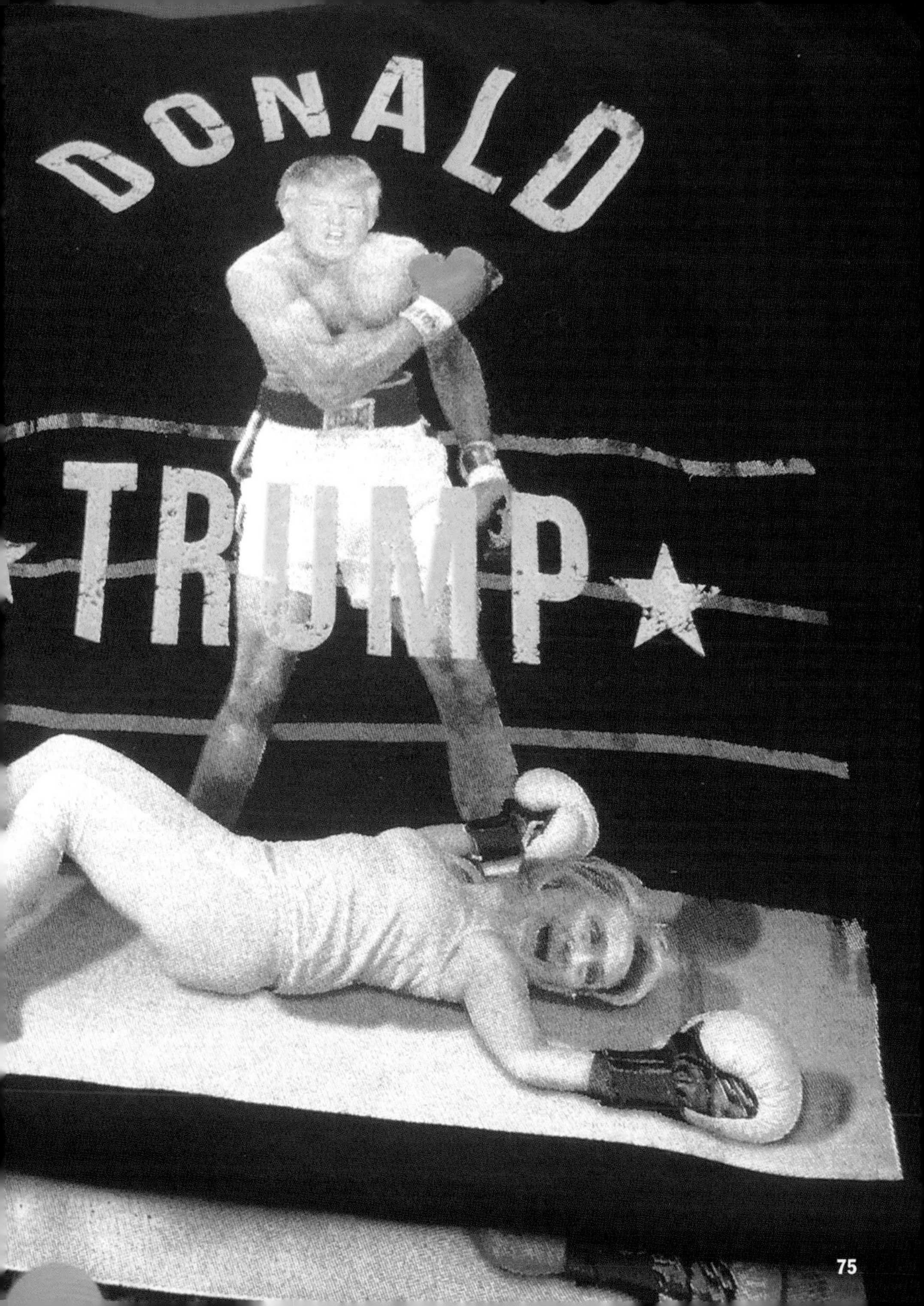
DONALD
TRUMP

77

Rope. Tree.
Journalist.

SOME ASSEMBLY
REQUIRED.

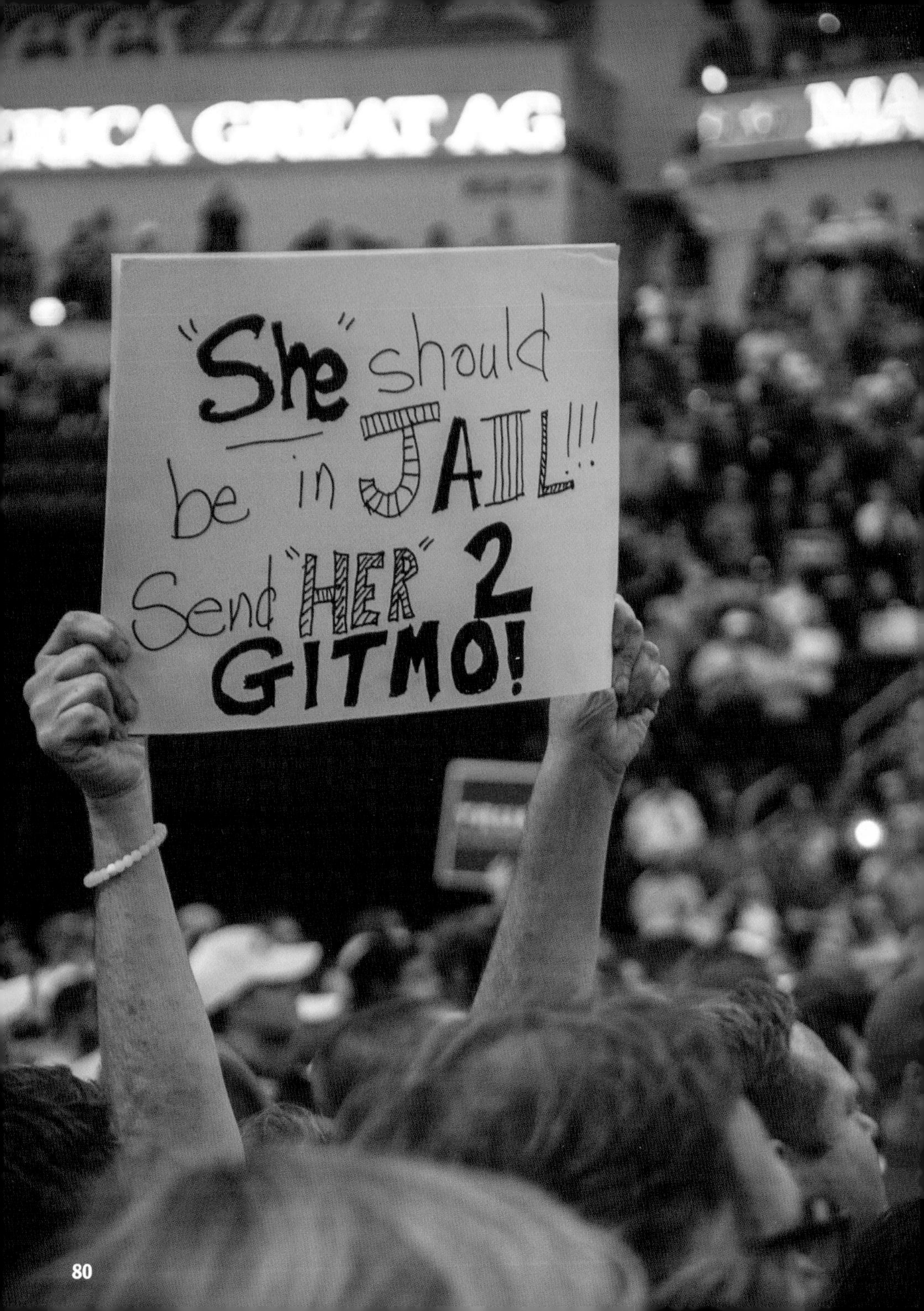
"She" should
be in JAIL!!!
Send "HER" 2
GITMO!

THE SECOND AMENDMENT

I PLEAD THE SECOND

BO

D

RS
FOR
M.P
E
ICA
AT
N!

BIKERS
FOR
TRUMP
MAKE
AMERICA
GREAT
AGAIN!

BIK
FOR
TR
MA
AMER
GRE
AGA

During 2016, "balls" became a popular word on pro-Trump political items, and the word was alluded to in stump speeches and debates by Republican candidates. "Finally Someone With Balls" and "We Need Someone With Balls" were popular slogans on Trump buttons and shirts. Other references to anatomy also appeared. "Don't Be a Pussy: Vote For Trump" signs were sold long before the Access Hollywood tape was released. Trump called Ted Cruz a "pussy" from the stage once, repeating the words shouted by a supporter. Some supporters wore shirts that called Clinton a "cunt." Marco Rubio famously mocked the size of Trump's hands during one speech. Trump responded during a debate by saying, "He referred to my hands, 'If they're small, something else must be small,'" he said. "I guarantee you there is no problem." During the general election, items praising Trump for having "balls" took on a dual meaning: balls signified toughness, but it was also a veiled statement against a female candidate.

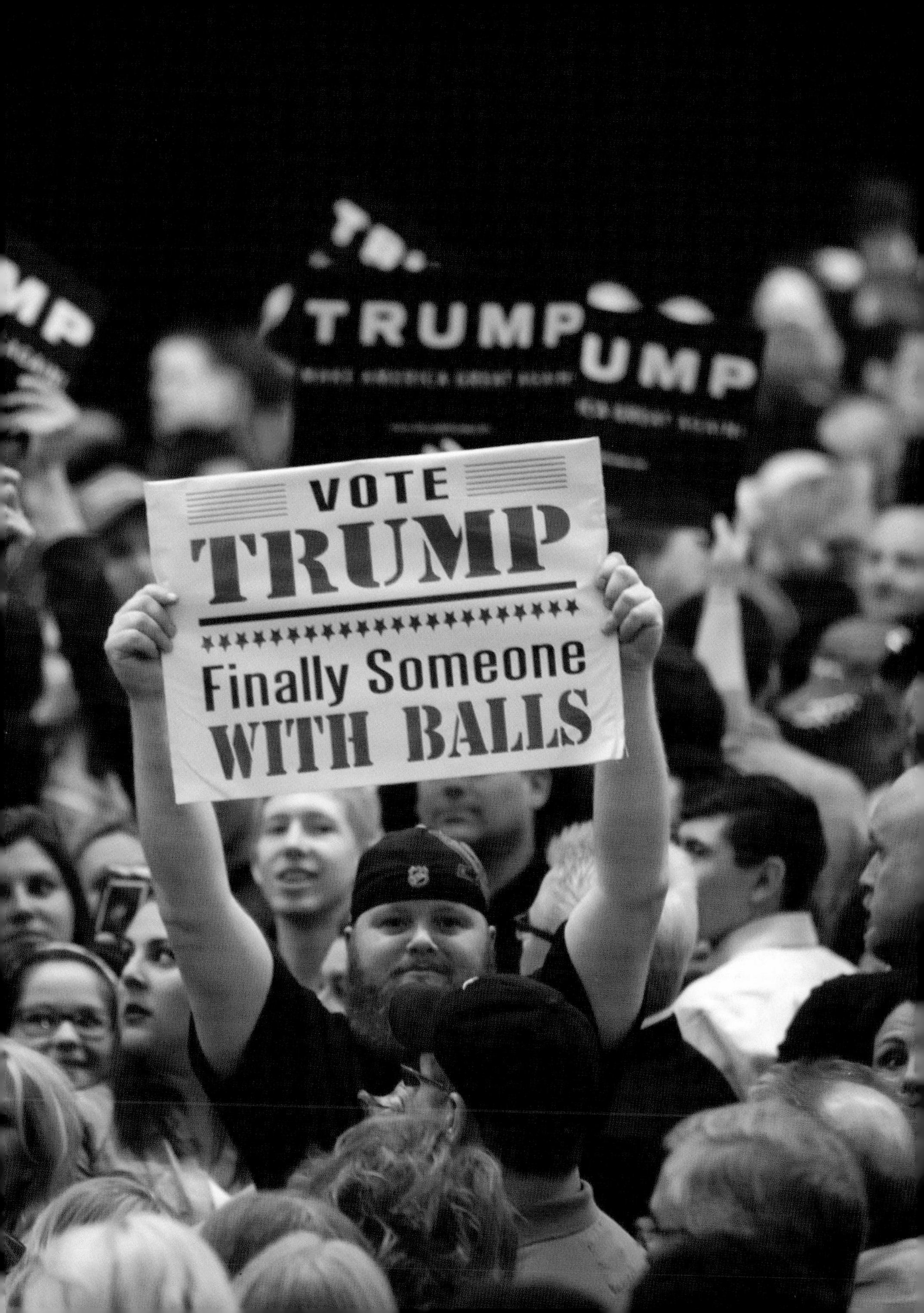
VOTE
TRUMP
Finally Someone
WITH BALLS
TRUMP

Donald *Fucking* Trump 2016

TRUMP ★ 2016 ★

MAKE AMERICA GREAT AGAIN

the silent majority
STANDS WITH
TRUMP

MAKE AMERICA GREAT AGAIN
★ ★ ★ ★ ★ ★ ★

HIL
SU
BUT NOT LIK
MONICA

A favorite jab at Hillary Clinton on campaign memorabilia was to attack her through Bill Clinton. His marital infidelity was referenced on many items. One of the most popular T-shirts on the campaign trail was "Monica Sucks, But Not Like Hillary." One bumper sticker for sale read, "If Hillary Can't Please Her Husband, She Can't Please the Country." As the warm-up speaker before a Trump rally in New Hampshire, former New Hampshire governor John Sununu said, "Do you think Bill was referring to Hillary when he said, 'I did not have sex with that woman?'" Following various sexual harassment allegations against Trump in the fall and the release of the Access Hollywood tape, a popular response from his supporters was to bring up past allegations against Bill Clinton by calling the former president a rapist.

Bill ton

KFC
HILLARY SPECIAL

2 FAT THIGHS
2 SMALL BREASTS
... LEFT WING

2 SMALL BREASTS
... LEFT WING

2 SMALL BREASTS
... LEFT WING

2 SMALL BREASTS
... LEFT WING

2 SMALL BREASTS
... LEFT WING

2 SMALL BREASTS
... LEFT WING

2 SMALL BREASTS
... LEFT WING

2 SMALL BREASTS
... LEFT WING

2 SMALL BREASTS
... LEFT WING

HILLARY SUCKS!
BUT NOT LIKE
MONICA!

fundbuttons.com

MADE IN USA

WITH
★ BALLS ★

Melania Trump
for FIRST LADY

DON'T TREAD ON
TRUMP

DON'T BE A CHUMP...
VOTE FOR
TRUMP

LIAR LIAR

BENGHAZI
Never Forget

BLUE

MAKE
AMERICA
GREAT
AGAIN!

VOTE NO
TO MONICA'S
EX-BOYFRIEND'S WIFE
IN 2016

NO
CA'S
WIFE
6

BI

AM

CRUZ BACK TO CANADA

HOT CHICKS VOTE TRUMP

★★★★★★★★★★★★★★★★★★★★★

If Hillary CAN'T please her HUSBAND,
She CAN'T please the COUNTRY!

VOTE TRUMP 2016

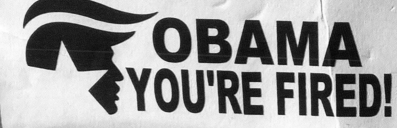

OBAMA YOU'RE FIRED!

Up
You

A backlash against political correctness and a celebration of crudeness was reflected in a wide variety of merchandise available at rallies. Some T-shirts worn at Trump events seemed designed for the purpose of shocking or offending. Trump's bashing of political correctness and his own use of profanity on the stage seemed to give his backers permission to bring out their own vulgar gear. The middle finger was on display during the 2016 campaign like never before in American electoral history. It was often directed at journalists, but the gesture also appeared on campaign items. One of the most popular buttons aimed to shock read, "KFC Hillary Special: 2 Fat Thighs, 2 Small Breasts ... Left Wing." This button first appeared at the California Republican Convention in 2013 where it was quickly removed, and the state party publicly disassociated itself from the vendor. The button re-emerged during the 2016 campaign, and it was widely available outside Trump rallies.

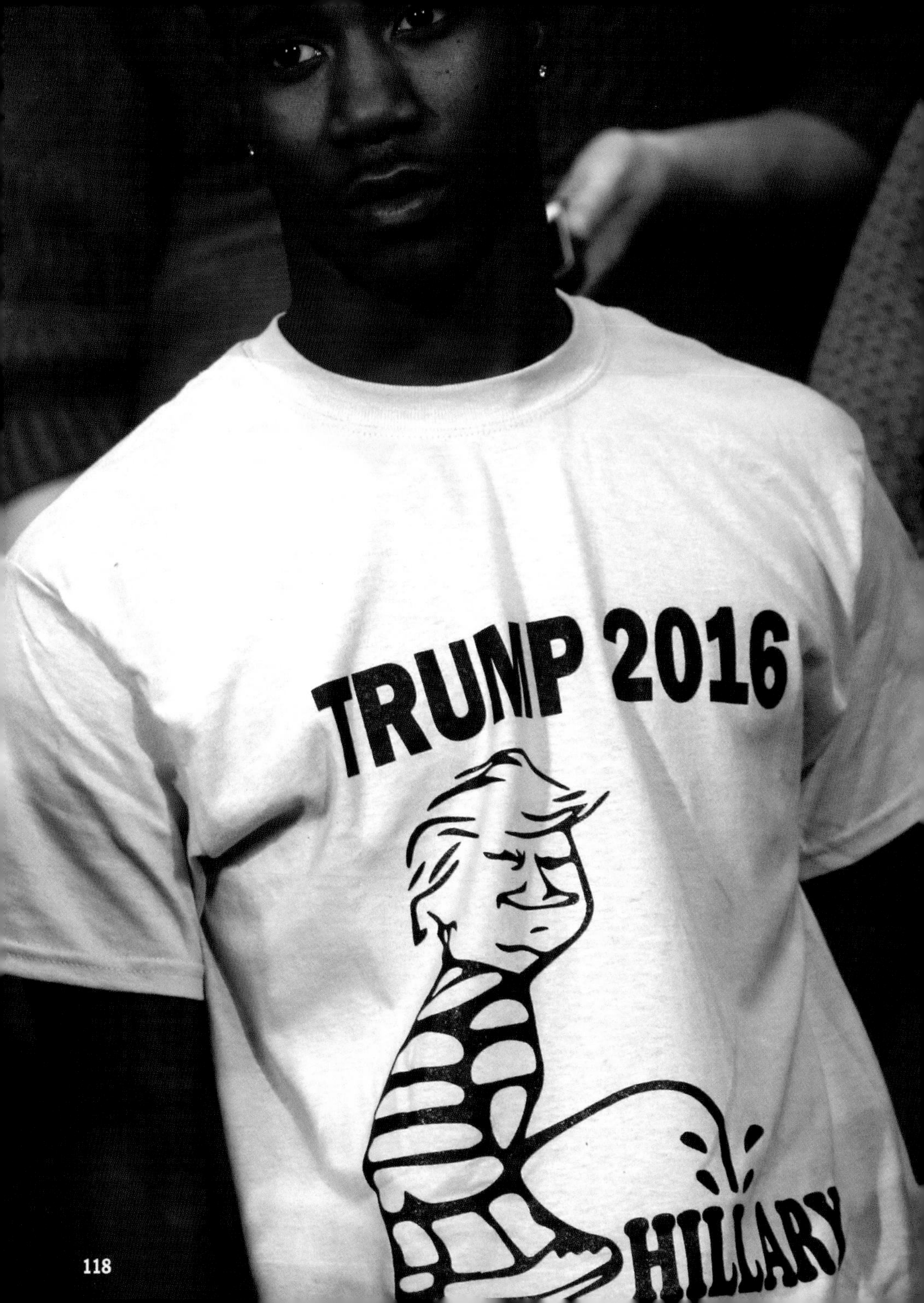
TRUMP 2016
HILLARY

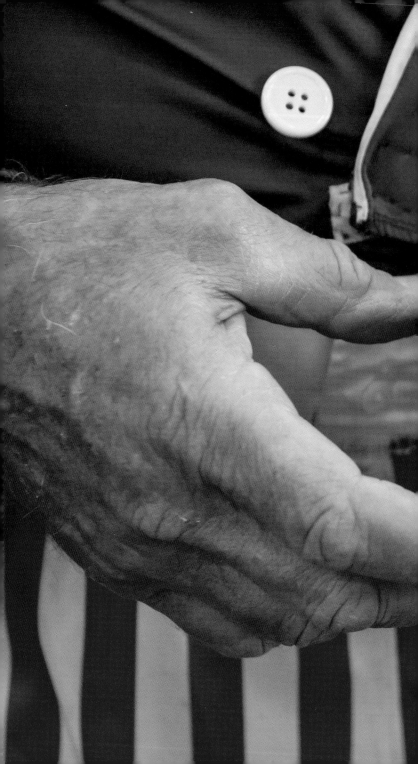

ONE WAY
F—K POLITICAL CORRECTNESS!
INMATE #11-13-33
GRAB HERE
BULLET PROOF VEST FUND

Rac

Confederate flags were one of the most outwardly racist items on display at Trump rallies. Merchants occasionally offered specially made Confederate flags that had "Trump for President" printed on them. In the parking lots around Trump rallies at certain venues, the flag could be seen flying on vehicles. The Trump campaign seemed conflicted about the flag. There are several examples of campaign staff asking supporters to remove Confederate flags hung at rally halls, but there are also examples of the flag being displayed prominently. The campaign allowed supporters to wear Confederate gear openly. It was common for buttons to mock the "Black Lives Matter" movement. There were many derivatives on the campaign trail, including "Deplorable Lives Matter". Unofficial merchandise also referenced Pepe the Frog, the cartoon character that became a symbol for the Alt-Right.

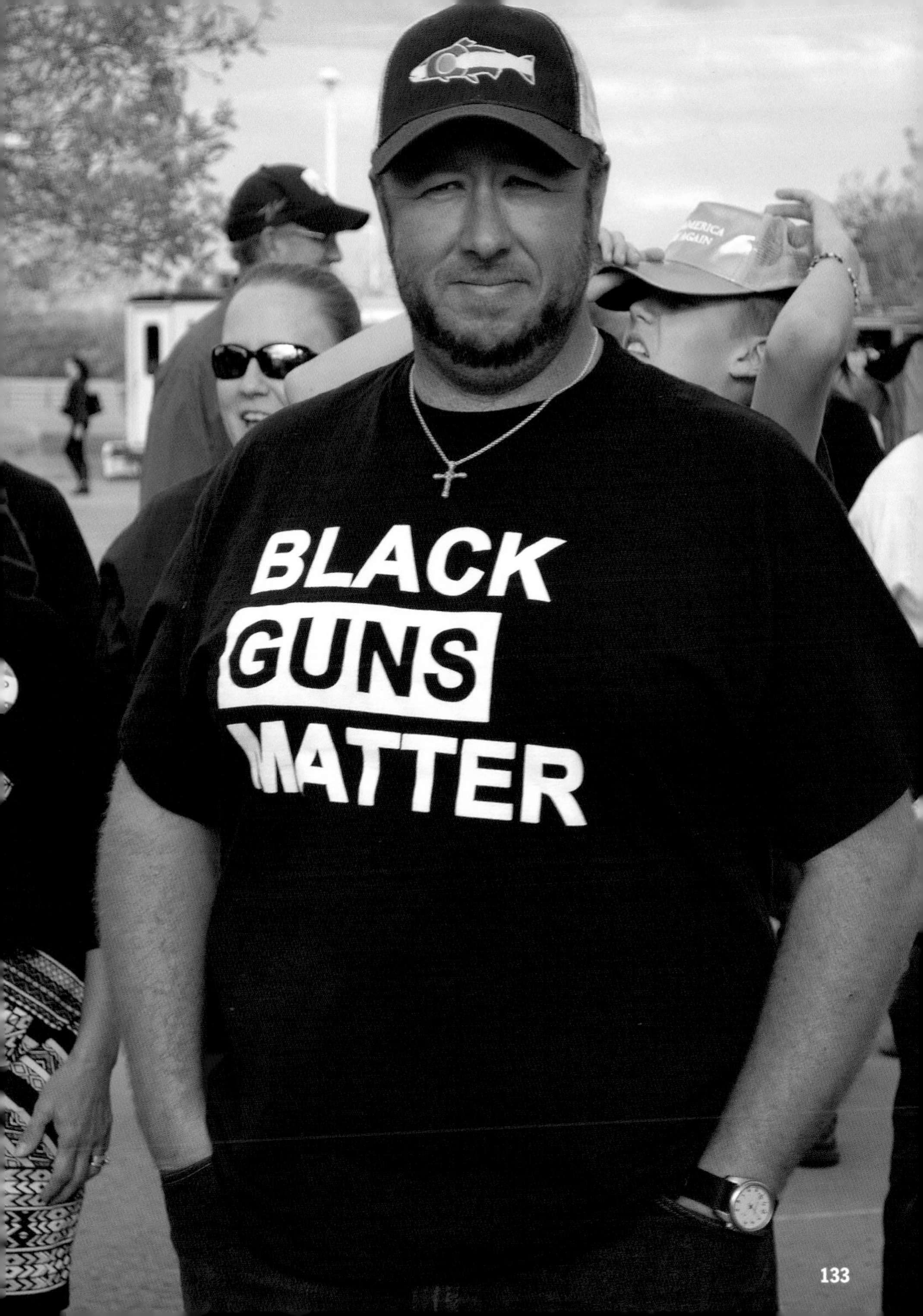
BLACK
GUNS
MATTER

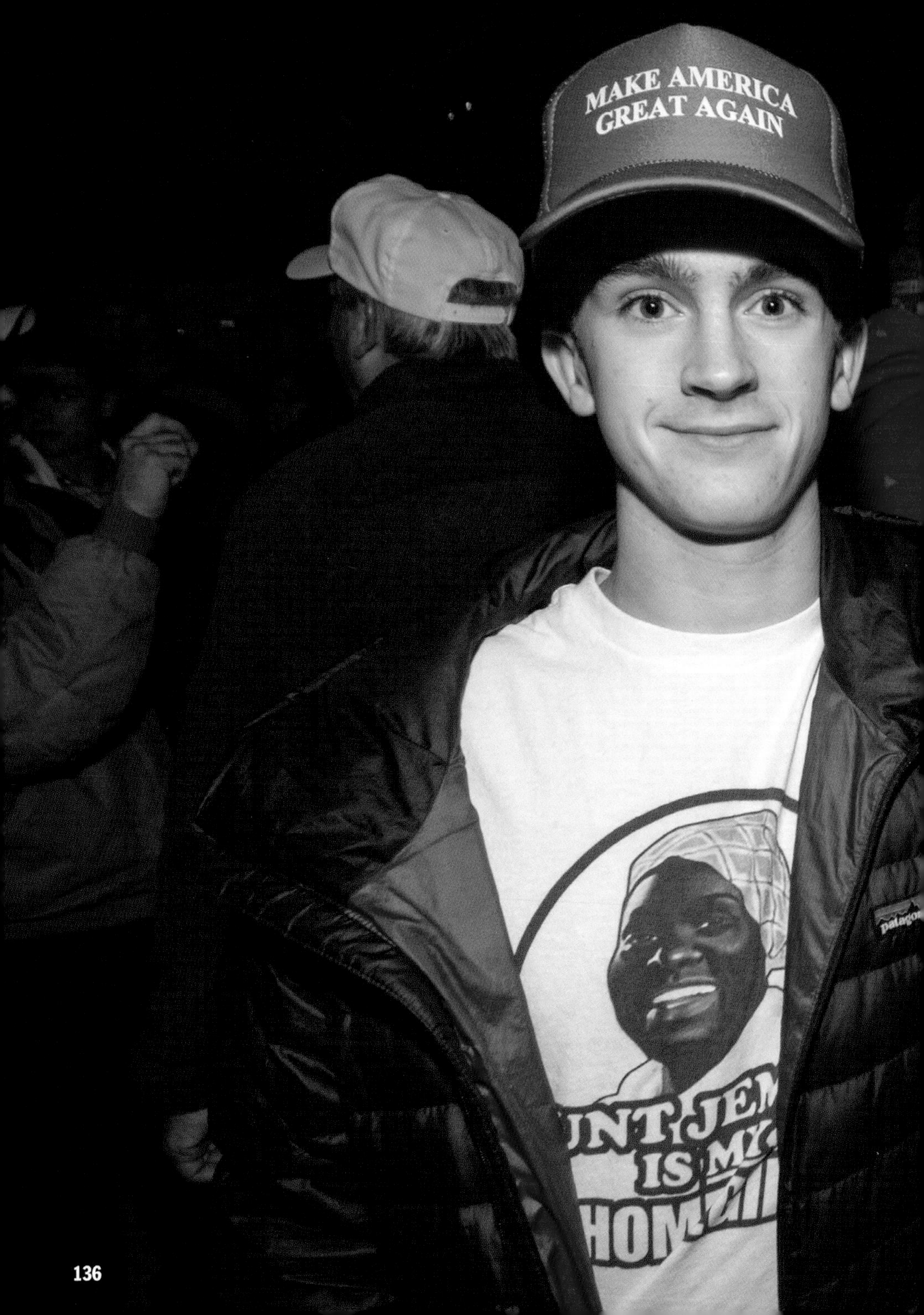
MAKE AMERICA
GREAT AGAIN

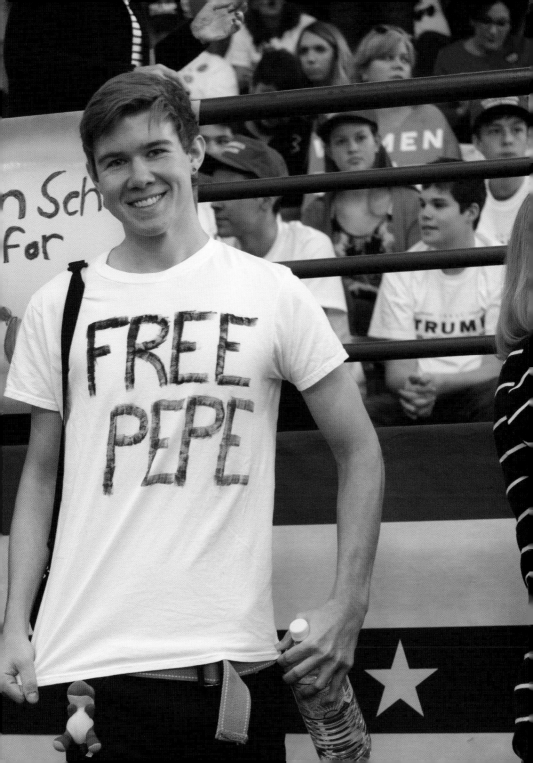

Dep

T-shirts and signs were the primary items that featured anti-immigrant and anti-foreigner messages. Some of the more extreme shirts seen at Trump rallies included "Muslims Suck," "Fuck Off We're Full," and "Islam Sucks." One button sold at rallies had the words "Build the Wall and Make Mexico Pay" with a drawing of a cartoonish, stereotypical Mexican wearing a sombrero saying, "Si Señor." The tamer "Build the Wall" buttons, shirts, and signs were the most common, along with "Get'em Out of Here" buttons.

port

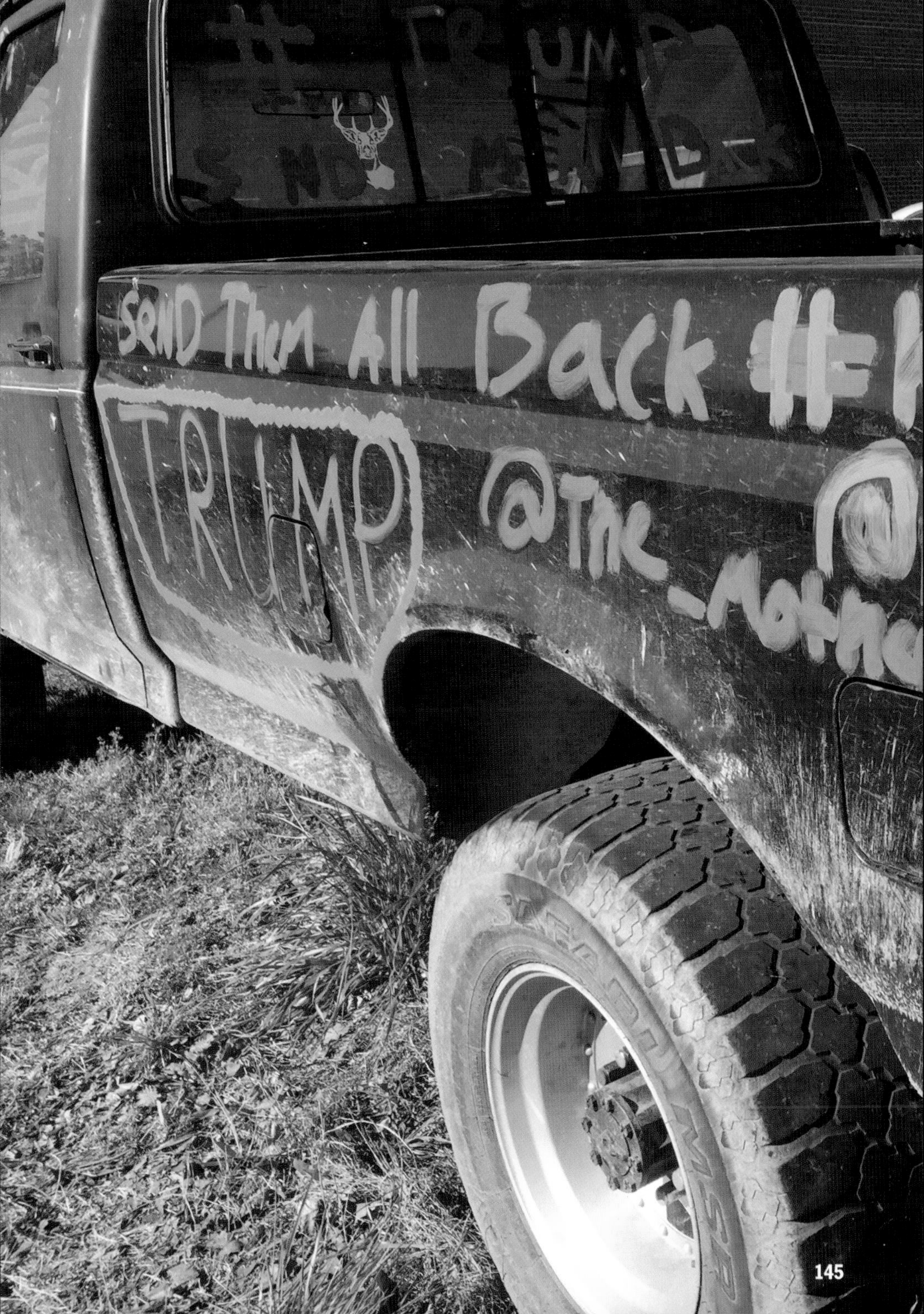
SeND Then All Back
TRUMP
@The

Evil

The portrayal of Hillary Clinton as evil and devilish was common on the campaign trail and took many forms. It served as a catch-all for all sorts of anti-Hillary attacks, some dating back to the 1990s. Hillary Clinton's image appeared with horns or fanged teeth in many places, along with the name "Killary." Trump played into this messaging from the podium as well. "She's the devil," Trump told a rally in August in Mechanicsburg, Pa. "It's true." For some supporters, these images had a religious undertone, while for others, the images had a tongue-in-cheek quality to them. References to the Benghazi incident were often made; merchandise often featured bloody handprints on top of a photo of Hillary Clinton's face.

WHAT DIFFERENCE DOES IT MAKE?
INFOWARS.COM

I came to the US legally!
Looking for the AMERICAN DREAM...
Not the MEXICAN NIGHTMARE!
Donald Trump 2016 MAKE MEXICO PAY FOR THE WALL!
LOVE! TRUMPS HATE
COME AND TAKE IT
HILLARY IS A DISHONEST,
UNTRUSTWORTHY, HATEFUL,
ABLISHMENT WHORE AND A ?ITCH!

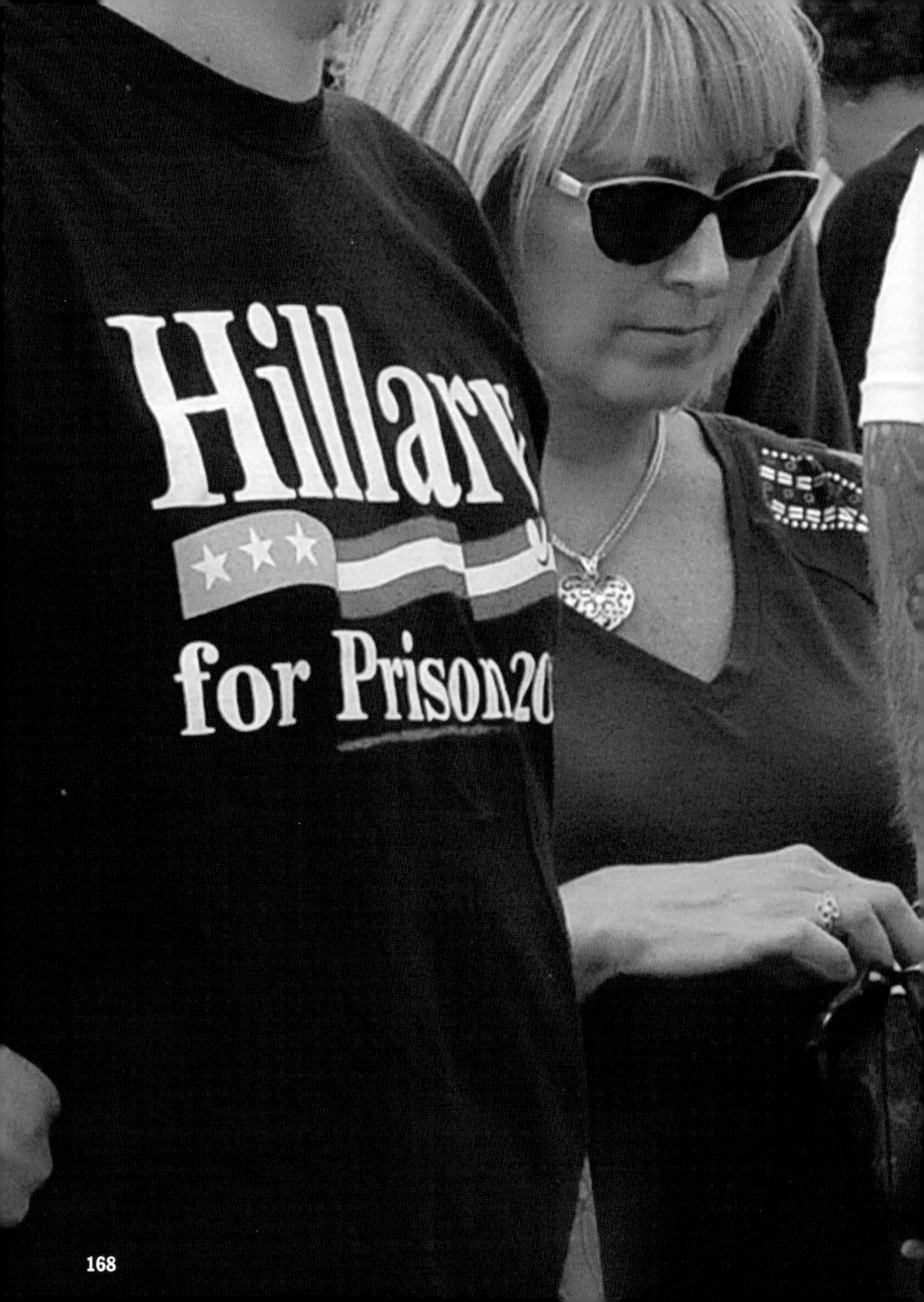
Hillary
for Prison20

Acknowledgements

This book would not have been possible without the generous support of 139 backers on Kickstarter. Their early support, enthusiasm and faith in this project helped transform the initial idea into a printed book. I would also like to recognize all the photographers, both professional and amateur, who have contributed images to this book. Finally, this book would not have been possible without the creativity and thoughtfulness of book designer Adam Hay.

About the Author

Paul Sherman is a writer, newsletter publisher, and conference producer with Tech Wire Media in Washington, D.C. He grew up in Austin, Texas, where he began political item collecting as a young boy. After graduating from Brown University in 1992 with degrees in Political Science and Latin American Studies, he worked as the news assistant at the Mexico City bureau of The New York Times for three years. He then worked as a freelance journalist for two years. In 1999, he earned an M.B.A. from The Wharton School. He lives in the Capitol Hill neighborhood of Washington, D.C. with his wife Kelly and two daughters. On weekends, he is often on the pool decks of swim meets or the sidelines of soccer games, cheering on his two daughters. He can be reached at www.paulsherman.com

Photography Locations

Page 7 (New York, NY), 12 (Cleveland, OH), 15 (Wilkes-Barre, PA), 16 (Sarasota, FL), 19 (DC), 20 (Henderson, NV), 23 (Leesburg, VA), 26 (Council Bluffs, IA), 28 (Manheim, PA), 29 (New York, NY), 30 (Orlando, FL), 32-33 (Cleveland, OH), 34-35 (Everett, Washington), 36-37 (Wilkes-Barre, PA), 38-39 (Sanford, FL), 40-41 (DC), 42-43 (Madison, MS), 44-45 (Tennessee), 46 (DC), 47 (Concord, NC), 50-51 (Bellmore, NY), 52-53 (Baton Rouge, LA), 54-55 (Hershey, PA), 56-57 (Concord, NC), 58-59 (Algonac, MI), 60-62 (DC), 64 (Phoenix, AZ), 65 (DC), 68-69 Virginia Beach, VA, 70 (Sarasota, FL), 71 (Tampa, FL), 72 (Virginia Beach, VA), 73 (Kinston, NC), 74-75 (Everett, WA), 76-77 (Los Angeles, CA) 78-79 (Minneapolis, MN), 80 (Hershey, PA), 81 (DC), 84-85 (Pittsburgh, PA), 86-87 (Henderson, NV), 88-89 (Johnstown, PA), 90-91 (Toledo, OH); 92-93 (Wilkes-Barre, PA), 94-95 (Macon, GA), 98-99 (Orlando, FL), 100-101 (Raleigh, NC), 102 (Prescott Valley, AZ), 103 (DC) 104 (Tampa, FL), 105 (Orlando, FL), 106 (DC), 107 (Berlin, MD), 108 (Hollywood, CA), 109 (Hershey, PA), 112-113 (Daytona Beach, FL), 114-115 (Cincinnati, OH), 116-117 (Cincinnati, OH), 118 (Ambridge, PA), 119 (DC), 120-123 (New Orleans, LA) 124-125 (Baton Rouge, LA), 128-129 (Macon, GA), 130-131 (Selma, NC), 132 (Buxton, NC), 133 (Loveland, CO), 134-135 (Pittsburgh, PA), 136-137 (Manchester, NH), 138-139 (Raleigh, NC), 142-143 (West Chester, OH), 144 (Sarasota, FL), 145 (Berlin, MD), 146-147 (Mannheim, PA), 148-149 (West Allis, WI), 150-151 (Anaheim, CA), 152 (Madison, AL), 153 (Miami, FL), 156-157 (Phoenix, AZ), 158-159 (Denver, CO), 160-161 (Northeast Texas), 162-163 (Concord, NC), 164-165 (Raleigh, NC), 166-167 (West Palm Beach, FL), 168-169 (Melbourne, FL), 170 (Gainesville, VA), 171 (Loveland, CO), 172 (Raleigh, NC)

Photography Credits

Page 1: Paul Sherman; Page 7: Everett Collection Inc./Alamy Stock Photo; Page 8 (top and bottom): Paul Sherman; Page 11 (all three buttons): Paul Sherman; Page 12: ZUMA Press, Inc./Alamy Stock Photo; Page 15 (rally photo): Sally Kohn; Page 15 (button): Paul Sherman; Page 16: Mandel Ngan/AFP/Getty Images; Page 19: Paul Sherman; Page 20: Robyn Beck/AFP/Getty Images; Page 23: Paul Sherman; Pages 26-27: Bob Daemmrich/Alamy Stock Photo; Page 28: Reuters/Mike Segar; Page 29: MediaPunch Inc./Alamy Stock Photo; Pages 30-31: Isabelle D'Antonio; Pages 32-33: Michael Reynolds/EPA/Newscom; Pages 34-35: Paul Christian Gordon/Alamy Stock Photo; Pages 36-37: Jonathan Alpeyrie/Polaris/Newscom; Pages 38-39: Paul Hennessy/Alamy Stock Photo; Pages 40-41: Rena Schild/Shutterstock.com; Pages 42-43: Julie Dermansky; Pages 44-45: ©Lynn Friedman 2016; Page 46: Paul Sherman; Page 47: Paul Sherman; Pages 50-51: Reuters/Stephanie Keith; Pages 52-53: Julie Dermansky; Pages 54-55: Zach D. Roberts/NurPhoto/Sipa USA/Newscom; Page 56: Paul Sherman; Page 57: Paul Sherman; Pages 58-59: Reuters/Rebecca Cook; Page 60: Paul Sherman; Page 61: Paul Sherman; Page 62: Paul Sherman; Page 64: @Gage Skidmore via CC (creativecommons.org/licenses/by-sa/2.0/); Page 65: Paul Sherman; Pages 68-69: AP Photo/Evan Vucci; Page 70: Mandel Ngan/AFP/Getty Images; Page 71: Paul Hennessy/Alamy Stock Photo; Page 72: Reuters/Jonathan Ernst; Page 73: Aude Guerrucci/Polaris/Newscom; Pages 74-75: Newzulu/Alamy Stock Photo; Pages 76-77: Alex Millauer/Shutterstock.com; Pages 78-79: Reuters/Jonathan Ernst; Page 80: ZUMA Press, Inc./Alamy Stock Photo; Page 81: Paul Sherman; Pages 84-85: Jeff Swensen/Getty Images; Pages 86-87: Robyn Beck/AFP/Getty Images; Pages 88-89: Stephanie Strasburg/Pittsburgh Post-Gazette 2017, All rights reserved. Reprinted with permission. Pages 90-91: Jonathan Alpeyrie/SIPA/Newscom; Pages 92-93: Sally Kohn; Pages 94-95: Grant Blankenship; Pages 98-99: Aftonbladet/ZUMA Press/Newscom; Pages 100-101: Tom Williams/CQ Roll Call/Newscom; Page 102: Pamela Au/Shutterstock.com; Page 103: Paul Sherman; Page 104: Paul Hennessy/Polaris/Newscom; Page 105: Paul Hennessy/Alamy Stock Photo; Page 106: Paul Sherman; Page 107: ©Amy McGovern under CC BY 2.0 (creativecommons.org/licenses/by/2.0/); Page 108: FiledIMAGE/Shutterstock.com; Page 109: Zach D. Roberts/ZUMA Press/Newscom; Pages 112-113: Paul Hennessy/Alamy Stock Photo; Pages 114-115: Reuters/Mike Segar; Pages 116-117: Caleb Hughes/Alamy Stock Photo; Page 118: Reuters/Mike Segar; Page 119: Paul Sherman; Pages 120-121: Julie Dermansky; Pages 122-123: Jose Bernaldo de Quiros; Pages 124-125: Julie Dermansky; Pages 128-129: Kevin D. Liles/kevindliles.com; Pages 130-131: Peter Eversoll; Page 132: Erin Kelly; Page 133: Chris Goodwin/desrowVISUALS; Pages 134-135: Reuters/Aaron Josefczyk; Pages 136-137: Andrew Cline/Shutterstock.com; Pages 138-139: Zach D. Roberts/ZUMA Press/Newscom; Pages 142-143: Brendan Smialowski/AFP/Getty Images; Page 144: Jennifer Wright/Alamy Stock Photo; Page 145: ©Amy McGovern under CC BY 2.0 https://creativecommons.org/licenses/by/2.0/ (photo cropped); Pages 146-147: ZUMA Press, Inc./Alamy Stock Photo; Pages 148-149: Jim West/Alamy Live News; Pages 150-151: mikeledray/Shutterstock.com; Page 152: Bob Gathany/Barcroft Media; Page 153: WENN Ltd/Alamy Stock Photo; Pages 156-157: ZUMA Press, Inc./Alamy Stock Photo; Pages 158-159: Chris Goodwin/desrowVISUALS; Pages 160-161: Bob Daemmrich/Alamy Stock Photo; Pages 162-163: Paul Sherman; Pages 164-165:Tom Williams/CQ Roll Call/Newscom; Pages 166-167: EPA/Cristobal Herrera/Newscom; Pages 168-169: Paul Hennessy/Alamy Stock Photo; Page 170: W. Mark Dyer; Page 171: Chris Goodwin/desrowVISUALS; Pages 172-173: Chip Somodevilla/Getty Images; Page 176: Paul Sherman.